CW01574542

suddenly, it's now

Blossom Hibbert

Leafe Press

Published by Leafe Press
Nottingham, England.
www.leafepresspoetry.com

Copyright © Blossom Hibbert, 2023. All rights reserved.
Cover photograph © Dale Hibbert, 2023. All rights reserved.

ISBN: 978-1-7397213-7-4

Cover photograph by Dale Hibbert

Contents

Thanks to the wise, old poets around me - who take coffee (black) and altruistically guide me.

Also to 'D' - this may not pay for our cafe on the shore, but is a start, nonetheless.

bedman

i can hear you through the walls, asking - who is this bedman of yours?
          unreachable within the milky way. hidden
          underneath a memory with his family of dust bunnies.

bedman is all the metaphors i cannot speak. too afraid of
          understanding the intrinsic, gaining all that self-awareness...
to whose benefit, for what
          use?

occam's razor suggests i define him as solipsism, but even that creates questions and raw spotless puddles. slight difference between mirror and water is blurred and far too close to differentiate, which is only as dangerous as identical twins   understand it to be.

bedman is negation of reachability. everything shunned, stuffed, twisted and hollowed into sentience. if you like, process human scepticism into tangible actions. create your very own
                                                            bedman!
i warn you. he cannot love.
          utterly incapable of devotion.
do not expect frank hands, back, shoulders.
do not expect absence of misery.

butcher holds paint-splattered knife. causes both grief and fullness,
complacency and excitement.   would rather starve
rotten bedman and me. lost him for quite a while. decades
even. ran away without saying
                                                            goodbye.

          spotting
                    his curious form
          plucking
                    his roadside shirt
          tucking
                    into   breast pocket

neighbours beside my beating fish.   gasp!
bedman watches me write all languid evening long, yearning to win my
cold heart over.   i never give in.
i never.
give. in.
[where did he come from?]
retired pianist

bought the lighthouse to live in across from puffin island. ran toward it
pulling gaunt backbone grand piano
beautiful sonatas   dropping onto
ten foreign cargo ships
sweating men on the docks swayed toward the ripping noise, wearing
medalled rain.
started as a novelty but within a week became common:
wood pigeon's coo-coo

workers' life frustratingly earnest. full of tempo and extensions, ripening
under the metronome sun. overly familiar with day's wild cycle. waking
just to see dawn   until
bedman didn't play anymore
[came running to me]

death: urban acupuncture to my deaf child, long since departed.

storm beaten lighthouse rotted inside out, generations of corduroy pants
and ropey chests followed him under. buried with sweet tasting bedman
memories.

what i mean is...   my retired pianist was forgotten. no - what i mean is,
if he can run away with nothing but a piano, i can run away with clock
tower loneliness. why did he come back to me, was he scared of a skirting
board society? what could be worse than
me?
[leading up to negation]

gap to bedroom became so small i couldn't squeeze back in. sent a mouse to retrieve my cold duvet. willing to caress and stroke and hold him with cursive trust. we could hide under moonlit covers together,
plotting.

stinking rodent never returned to my arms.
felt loneliness, betrayal, heartbreak all in one bucket. slammed car door on finger of love. slept with carrots and single aubergine. thought i participated a lot that night to the conversation. signed love sheet, promised not to spill any beans. froze myself into boxed sleep. tricked into believing the world around me was expand i n g. dreamt of tiny letterboxes covering large red door and managed to wiggle myself inside one, looking for

bedman got stuck

squished woke upright telegram of flesh

think next morning was a sunday, arised as near to the percolator as possible... score! climbed out white fridge of revolution.
bedman coughed phlegm onto my naked feet, soon sent him packing. watched next door's crazed child steal cigarette pack off the counter and a gallon of milk from the milk stream. called police all by myself, proud officers arrived ever so promptly. three paper weight boys stood in someone's kitchen, let themselves in.

bedman hitched a ride.

[four men loitered]

thought of them as i wept over flowers for algernon. kept receiving advice from someone. stored inside tiny metal tin sat on mantelpiece.
bedman took them straight out and ripped everything up. childish revolution, after all he is the

KING OF YOUTH.

that night, dreamt in zeros and iced finger buns.
[searched inside sink for bedman]

[static]

what actually happened? beside low thready pulses, liver struggling with last night's overdose and the imaginary goat needing a walk, not a whole bunch of bananas.

must be off then. getting early [watch]

will you be mine again, after all our time apart? guts no longer belong to me, who governs this decision? what if intestines get replaced by a coil of red ribbon, who would ever even

know?

[conversationconversationconversation]

spent the day an exhausted blocked toilet, kept flushing but just spilled out, chronically regurgitating. unable to swallow. throat locked up for the night [hostile behaviour]. closed red eyes
fell asleep. awoke as the worm in adam's apple.
awoke in bedman's utter absence.

suddenly, it's now.

whole days

but we are miles apart and your thoughts
are not of me whilst i cannot call your
          arm back
spending whole days
remaking your sudden face. pulled into a
junction all   shoulder crack spleen
          sliced bacon on bedside table

paper café folds itself neatly into quarters
fitting perfectly in arched man's pocket
          stomach rumble
          order coffee just for biscuit
          leap into street of hopelessness
vacant houses cry to be touched but everyone is afraid of deserted
solitude and dying alone with

[single egg on toast]

          surely, this cannot be ?

other land

you know, it is the wind that will kill me in the end
i will try and follow it until i have trodden
on black soil on   your corner of the earth
drop right down the cold side
                penultimate breath
leaving that bitter body of mine

you know, i will be death in the end
we can meet up in the
                                other land
where there is no breeze at all
where street lights
want to switch on
        where
we sit together again and
bless this stagnant air, following

morning prayer of
        two atheists
sat side by side
        [singing]
        [praying]
        [weeping]

having a bath with you

yes.   world is rotating but tiger never
misses his prey and you
   wearing blue trousers, eventually
stop touching my faded painting
yes.   man in wet bath is leap frog
cold ears sticking out low clouds
yes.
          assess risk.
arm is a
swan's neck, well
swim toward him
                  then

circumstances

men drink white tea and
            women black coffee
table legs strain with weight of all these old books
mug handles   clunk and
                                        toast crumbs sit between pages

large nose presses against the window

drizzle

open the wound stick the moon in it
how was the blackest sea? did it rain?
it didn't rain here.   lakes inside the
moon stayed well put. wet
is a state of mind i cannot   shift
are you waving at me, are you
waiting at the buttoned
                                        shoreline?
                    [i was such a fool]

this chair will not abandon me partly because it never had me
partly because i do not let it
sublimely indifferent to whether i exist or [ ]
poet is one who de-familiarises the world, wakes only to see the
          dawn.
                    [silence as moon goes into labour]

living just to get attached, is that so? cannot write without
wrenching solitude,
dull old habit of mine. i should stand on it really i should squash it
right down   till i am stood in your room inside muscled rain
                    till i can't even remember

why i wanted to sit on that
                                        chair
in the dark rotten first place

bats in the room above

sometimes lying on your bed
                    inside a languid afternoon
underneath top floor bats
          rented from some   socialite
you knew from time since   lost

whilst you are out on shift, i think to split an atom
exactly in half. hiding under freshly milked sheets
          watching how far apart
each half can fight
until universe collides inside bullet holes
          and you
dinnerless, dependable, dirty

come running back to find me

goose

no evidence to prove i exist today
my love   my what?
goose came waddling down the street and not very soon after a fox,
but soon enough to warrant my questioning of existence
                                               my what?
police sirens, choral singers, dark leafy green unfurling
        [dusk envelopes the day]
because... my love   my what?

light negates all hope of change
        we stagger through morrow day

the leaf is full and swollen now

call

you call me from the storm and tell me you are worried
your cat didn't come home last night
i try to console the most sensitive side of our partnership
pull hat over ears and sob inside a rainy day

you hang up the phone

glenmorangie in the station

and yet
door hinge creaks with reluctance to let the outside in. and yet
i left you on the back end of a sigh, muddled within the wreckage of
your own doing
and yet   i do not even know where you came from!
you obsolete thing, you. eating words in front of me, challenging me
to a battle of silhouettes neither you
nor i can see
        [that'll be the whisky]
and yet
chewing a big breakfast. finishing words of pleasant obligations
        [start with big things move on   quick]
walk a canal's length of discussion
                retire to stoic snuffed out sleep
and yet. perhaps. everything was all grey. or perhaps [more likely]
you forgot to warn me about tasty salvation
                                        and yet!
it was all about sipping
warm glenmorangie
                [beside you]
in the station

for my eyelids

the shape of a stick confuses me or
        confusion sits in the shape of a stick
we have drunk ourselves silly it is   peculiar
lungs thought they would feel something by now
i'll stop depriving things of oxygen if you stop asking me questions of
        canals and russell avenue
[brave fire. cord sliced.   blood, greet kitchen knife]

        peanut butter on green skirt surprising no one
write down your number in red on a napkin make me create a
hypothesis of desire we can work side by side
        [do not]
call me on that number.   leave a landline postal address your
coordinates as low as the old crow flies, feign interest in disbelief of
        politicians. wind blows secrets out of damp pockets.

when i grow up i want to be a postman greengrocer fisherman
        sports presenter
side business of   ...   rug store.
naked skin and delivering fragile veins. birthmark on ring finger
        [hurrah, lets marry off the baby!]

melancholy thursday, it is   time to retire it is
        lunchtime to retrieve
livestock popping up from blue grass, pure and possessing astounding
beauty only   ruminants own.
cows are better at thinking than me. better at sticking around wildman
street   than me.
thinking is incredibly difficult. squeeze brain/ wring
heavy cloth at bottom of sink
everything slips down the drain but chunks remain

yours, mouldy plum in the room above.

try to establish permanence, fail

raise eyes, turn all mourning radio stations on.

tune in to tiny's lullaby wearing small clothes. pass
on that - thanks. take shirt off   clean!
          beckoning soul
fertile land inside cracked skull, you
green thumb, green sleeves, tune in to
tiny's lullaby [pass]. why do i call on   [god]
in times of greatest need?

different lover
          compare death with dreamland
trying lover
          try to establish permanence
                    fail

wondering why you dont know where i am
forgotten your face, you
          know
eating cold salmon in chair green
                    watching metal seahorse circle
he is getting further than me not heading back to the hotel
          [with me?]
not heading anywhere   with me

sleep
          pass
                                        fail.

magnesium

i only want to read my book and sleep and run and buy magnesium by the
          bucket load
writing - smudged mirror chasing me down sand speckled road
          horizontal author who
sips and puffs and writes their way into pregnant afternoon
sometimes
                    breaking for
gulp of fresh air   mug of cold water
sometimes   just
keep writing until [ ] knocks on
ten days since i last saw you and who hasn't
                    moved?
voice behind the door says: where are you
          patiently, i wait.
there is no answer but
          sun replies
do not move! excited at the prospect of growing taller
often i get lonely i am such bad company
          at times
pouring into my mind a list of things i can do with this
                    new found height
everything is the same as yesterday. i smell my shoulder and start again

          binman puffs past. amble, amble... soldier

solipsism of the morning

breakfast eggs
sliced by willing sailor
six black ships arrive
solipsism slips on
ugly naked ugly feet
it is concerningly late, again.
knitted jumper playing billiards for blue eyes only. truthful and
silent and entirely weak
i do not sleep well but
who does anymore?
orange lights woosh over the train tracks on the ceiling, provincial
station i sit and sip inside
watch dark reds take the first train out, gripping bacon rolls and
eternal
americanos
wheezing into next shift next century next everything is the same
and precious my bed is warm from one belly button

can it be true, that i do not sleep well?
cold morning knocks on front door.
cushioned socket answers
transistor radio in angel hand, mother i am
afraid i do not sleep very well anymore

i put your jumper on and leave the house.

five

clock mutters five.
        dreamt i held you. dreamt i had the biggest hand in the world and held your neck
        safely pining   awfully   resistible

clock whispers five.
        writing my testimony under damp sheets. kindling for dead fire that became too familiar so received a whack

clock writes five, stubbing expressive stick out on   thigh
god forbid what i'd do

            if i had a half decent dog to walk

dear dearest

dear dearest, what did you have for breakfast and did you feel
very much alone?
dawn chorus is gutters slotting in and out as rubbish trucks take
warmth to work and squawks of infected magpie rattle rattle
shapes live forever inside blackfriars. collecting lighters
from northern floor, leading me to that higher place. believe
[romance] bright holy buses spit
grumpy babies onto workplace pavement
fingers are empty if they can't have you they can't have anything
but honest soap and water. microcosm of wakefulness splashes her
indoor face, pane of glass i am looking through is double-glazed
beach combing. it gives me happiness or perhaps just not
sadness

dear dearest, why aren't you here to protect me?
is this what i think it is. man might wrongly wonder. pupils drawn
to rotten wetness dying behind his bins in the early hours of
my morning. collecting two tins of black sludge
for the weary daybreak travellers. return to her warm prairie,
cowboy. bell singing boots and whitman's sliding love call on the
overused telephone, grey sky paradise till we slurp upward.

kitchen and breakfast room announcement: poetry is dead!!
wood thronged throat bubbles out of ant hills drowned by late
night vice whilst he, longing for his dead father
[as i now long for you] scratches filthy neck. knows you cannot
be innocent and be loved
[yawns beside my guts]

dear dearest, i miss you fondly. i'll be home before you know it, get
some good sleep into you.

on: nearly time

on: the other side of coming home
by your side could never   quite   slot
          give me hard tight words. i will be friends with only
truth. pick splinters out of the mess we made, push them into
                    vulnerable bitten fingers
sit at walls window and fall asleep in a
brown chair. think of nothing but what to feed the birds when
sleepily rising from the earth's core
          movement is reversed clocks out of control
          curving beside your frustrating denial

how long is your coat now, does it grow with age?
has it been three years now, or   four?
how old are you   and
                    are you growing old in the night?

          do you still have back pain?

old book

i say, i think we should start reading to each other in the dark times.
i say, we should start selling coffee grounds to the pope who
comes to the door every wednesday evening. pulling his soggy hand
through slow traffic lights, underneath crumble bridge then say
come on, come on quick – you must go find an old book to read to
me when the candles are lit.
does not react.   places pity on me under a rain hat.

we go to an op-shop where boys hold their nose because sofas
smell like sneeze, he looks for an old book to read to me when stars
shine wild and galloping. watch his bare hands take a book with
honesty of grandeur
flips few pages, snaps shut, slots back.   searches again.
repeats this over and over and over again.
pity him with wilted eyebrows and wonder about cold coffee dregs
sat stagnant inside the cat back home. think to ring of scum with
pawprint inside, hum to myself about angel cakes.
rain lingers on.

wet is satisfied in its own corruption of the sky; causing everything
to sag, holding soft-egg virtue. leaves give in to greedy pull of
gravity and branches ask me: where is he? heart drips out empty
arms.

that man is the trainline version of an emperor.

leaving him alone to pick out old book, feet walk to bench.
rest tired spine, sit and suck and ruminate. watch guitar
with fingers and unattached thumb, neck hidden from private
officers inside shirt collar. baby stumbles around the way they
always do and undergrown fingers reach into the air, splayed out
and shrugging: where is he? wonder if someone reads to her in the
evening time.
bench is wet. i am   waterproof.
think to the currency of happenings, baby stares at me, still young
enough to think the entire point of ageing is self-realisation; also,

the way women look at other women. **pity.**

baby has become such an integral part of my vision and scattering
inside my head forces heart to pulse to throat at the thought of
        either leaving. [please   don't leave]
panic swells cymbal crashes. pity assumes a moss position. first
arrival at the forgotten stone door, waiting for the flood.

        rain eases up and sun pushes clouds apart, laughing.
he comes back from the store that smells like pea soup and
Bolsheviks, holding a yellow <u>old book</u> about boats.

drinking dawn side hot coffee hits my chest and i am warming up, in
the way a fleshy glorified toilet tube knows how to do best.
        sit next to me, on the horizon. teeter beside me.
his back a metal shield against rest of nasty world.

inside me, a feeling grows. hmm... twitching and twisting and turning
and travelling into something
                                glorious!

recover from heavy illness. view life for first time   ever.
the appreciation is oh so burdening and sickening yet... most
marvellous one of all. i am pushing strength back into sick, swollen
bones.
        lungs, please vacate all that heavy mucus.
                        eviction notice: now!

the whole time you've been thinking of the word 'feather' you've felt
both fear and terror. isn't that strange? something so light and fragile
that can be stolen with a hiccup... equating to a mountain of disquiet.
isn't that   so   strange? feel not as if i am missing organs but
instead, too many stuffed inside. not sure who i am or where to go
next. lucky to own three beating hearts.
what happens when a walking stick gets caught in the spokes of
        my wheel and it stops. stops. stops?
        stops.

are you there, old book?

struck by the peculiarity of membranes separating me into compartments, forging a life out of mud and plastic toys and blades of grass. smells like dirt and heavy piss but

it's mine.

i don't mind.

it's my own mind, minding my life within dark body of membranes. waiting for plastic hands to be touched by something of substance.

[he doesn't]

too busy waiting for baby to fall over. music creates tiny fluctuations in the secret bone hidden in my ear. bone which isn't made of calcium, but youth and mercury: buzzing transmitter.

[baby is grandma reincarnated]

i am strange and mysterious and increasingly under the care of god. pity me *not* because sun has gone behind the clouds and the soft world is sleepy, but because back is moving towns. pity me *because* i am losing a shield ---- me for i am in the middle of a battleground, naked .

music abruptly   stops.

PITY ME! why should i?

grandma no longer stumbles. scooped into protector's muscled, holy arms. removed from the fight. pity the bourgeois baby for she is not allowed to yield a machine gun and fight for her people, pity her – not   me.

focus not that someone else has thought of a glorious **big** thing – but instead on the interesting **little** things that are rattling in your head. a coin in the washing machine. tu-tu, tu-tu.

old book gets caught in my throat;   cannot   ...

swallow. (pity froths out mouth)

grateful to be able to use my nose to breathe today.

pity pages because they are covered in saliva and enzymes and alphabetical profanities.

man puts me in his pocket, takes me home and reads to me in the evening times.

sitting happily in his pocket alongside 2p coin,
marble, crust of bread and mother's
        eulogy. boiler brews, cold fingers deep ocean diving
showing me off
        his insane cat, crazy with lust for the fellow

we will sell our coffee grounds to the pope who comes to the front door on a wednesday. through grit salt teeth and thin lips. times are hard now. we must remove the **darkest** things.

he will remain alone and when his cat eventually dies he'll come to rely on me as the walking cane in the spoke of his bike wheels
                and so...
<u>old book</u> is thrown into a large hole and covered with wet soil. dirt
sticking to letters, fringe on wet forehead. i will learn that i can
survive without 'important' things. we will pity the pope with his
second-hand weak coffee. he will pity me like i pity him. soil is filling the
hole up nicely now, covering it   tightly. ch, ch chhh....

shovel is a tool in the game of life. soil his darkest hour of redemption. if only it had snowed, we wouldn't be in this ghastly, DARK situation. pity.

suddenly, it's now.

Ingram Content Group UK Ltd.
Milton Keynes UK
UKHW020317080623
423046UK00011B/189

9 781739 721374